A School of Fish

Written by Michèle Dufresne

PIONEER VALLEY EDUCATIONAL PRESS, INC.

Here is a fish.

Swish, swish, swish!

The fish uses its **tail**

and its fins to swim fast.

scales
head
gills
fins

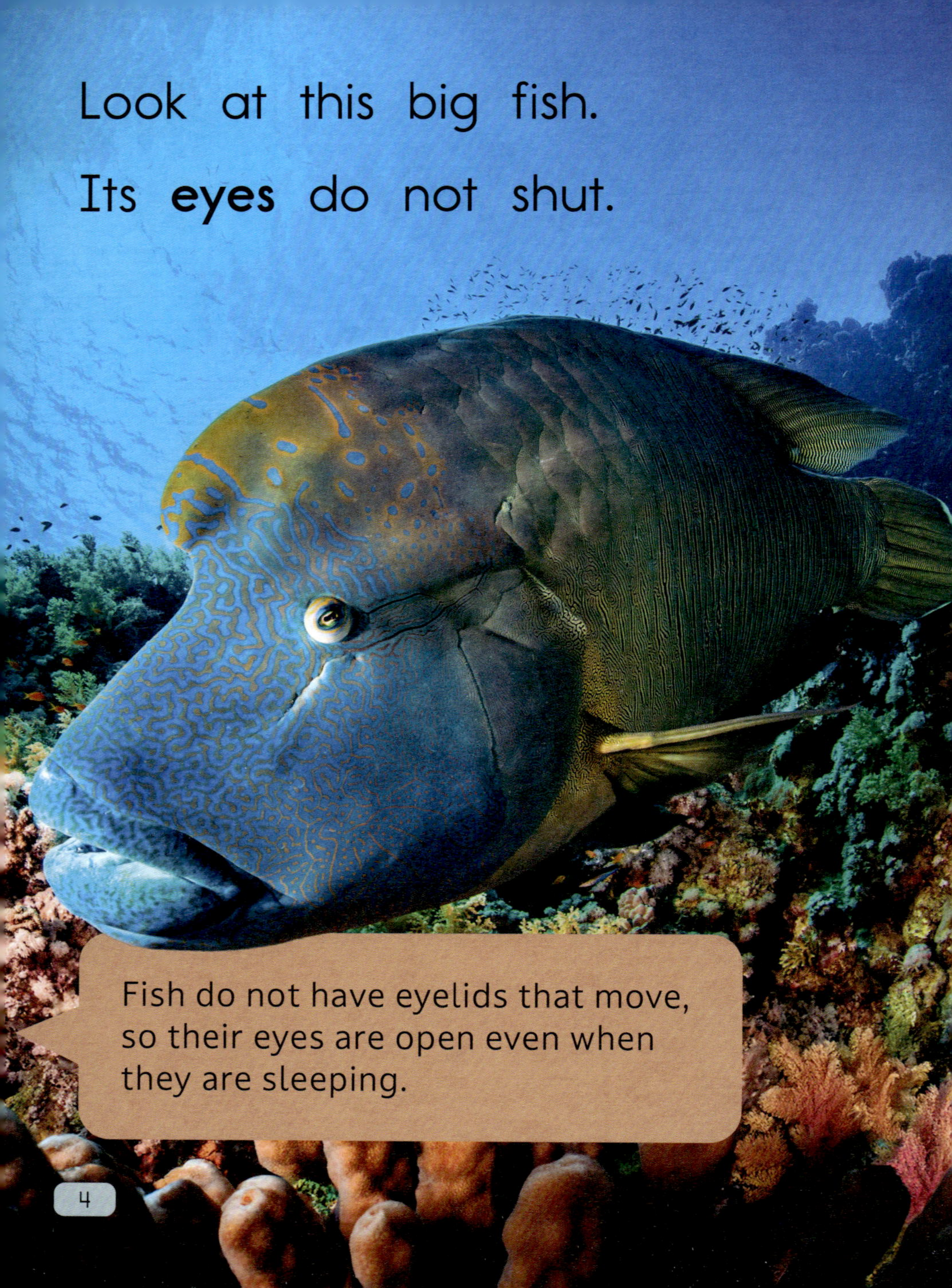

Look at this big fish.

Its **eyes** do not shut.

Look at the fish.
The fish swim in and out
of the ship.

Shipwrecks deep on
the ocean floor are
home to many fish.

Do you see a flash?

It is a **lanternfish**.

Lanternfish have glowing blue-green lights running down their sides that can flash on and off. This allows them to signal each other in the dark.

Look out!

This fish can shock you.

It is an **electric eel**!

Electric eels are not aggressive and will not attack unless cornered.

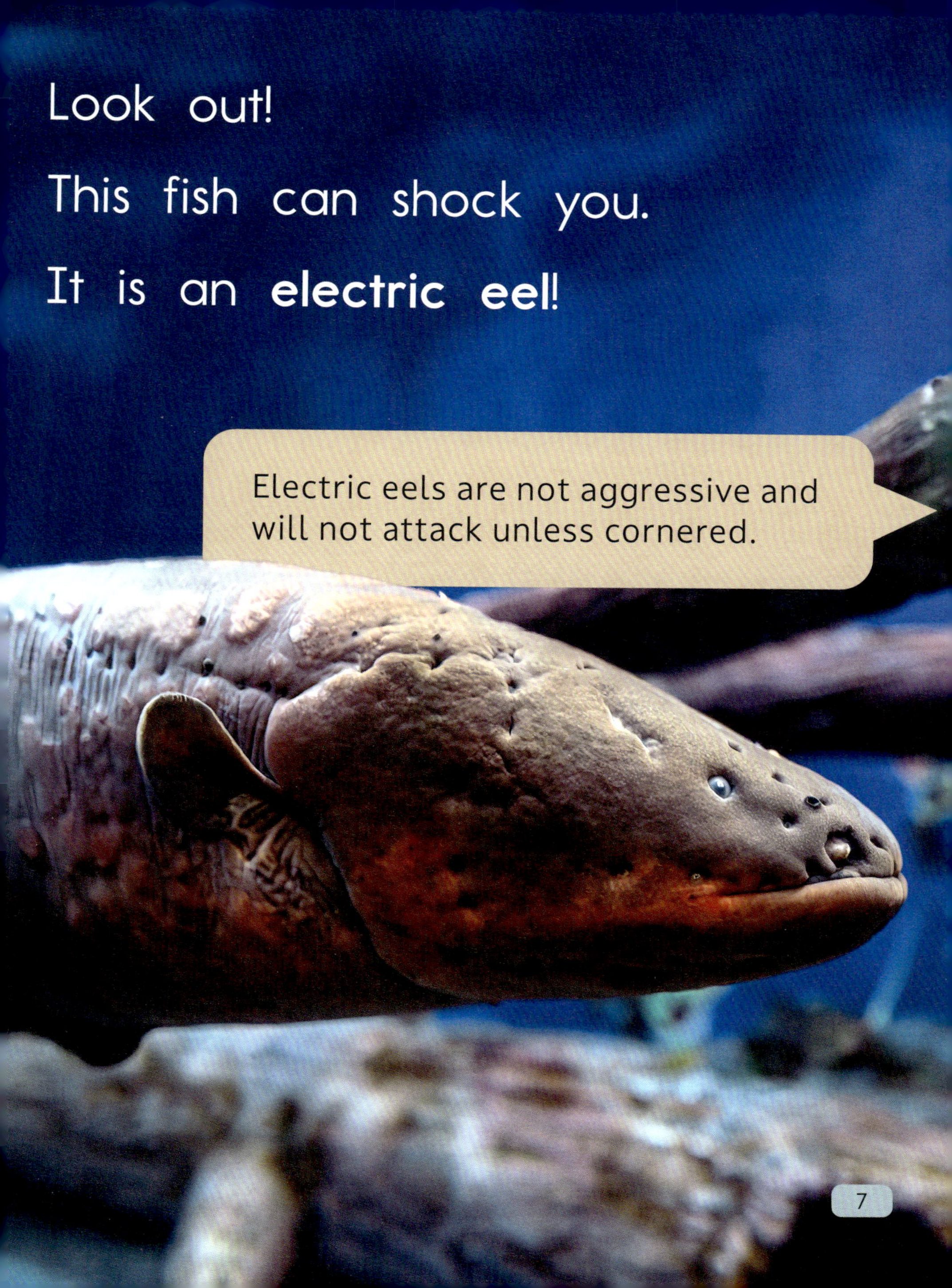

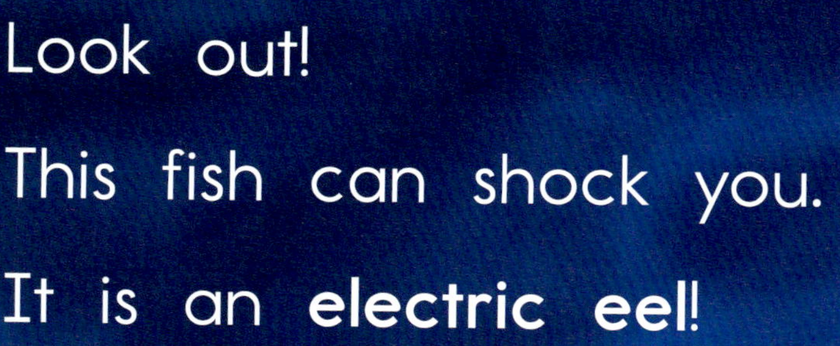

This is a bass.
Bass like to swim
in fresh **water**.

Bass live in bodies of fresh water like lakes, rivers, and ponds.

Can you see the trash
in the water? Trash is not
good for fish.

Many fish mistake trash, such as plastic, for food. This is very harmful to fish and to people who eat fish as well.

glossary